DOWN THE GARDEN PATH
Cold Porcelain Flowers

A constant source of inspiration, every day my garden rewards me more than I deserve for the time I have been able to put into it. The buttercups and the nettles however, are never far from the path just to keep me on my toes!

FIRST EDITION - October 2012

Published by A M Reynolds Publishing
The Yews, Lein Road, Kingston on Spey
Fochabers, Moray IV32 7NW

ISBN No. 978-0-9571554-1-1

Copyright © Alyson Reynolds

A catalogue record for this book is available from the British Library.

Written by Alyson Reynolds
Design and Layout, Photography and Drawings by Alyson Reynolds © 2012
Printed and Bound by MMS Almac Ltd, Keith, AB55 5DD

All flowers and arrangements contained within this book have been made by the author

Contents

Introduction

A warm welcome to my 2nd book 'Down the Garden Path'.

This time the inspiration has come from my own garden. A 'Cottage' style garden which constantly evolves through the seasons offering snapshots of colour and lasting impressions. Nothing really fancy, just good old fashioned garden flowers that often get overlooked for their more exotic cousins.

Through the varied subjects within, I hope to be able to share with you different techniques which will give you more knowledge to develop your skills and apply them to make many other flowers. It is not always easy to put instruction into words, so I have included step by step photos to help with the translation.

From Magnolias to Sweet Peas, Hydrangeas to Wall flowers, Goldenrod and Philadelphus to Escallonia, Helleborus, Poppies and many more, there is plenty of difference in structure and colour to absorb. All these flowers can be displayed in a variety of ways and I have included some photographic suggestions at the back of the book to demonstrate.

Trust your own judgement especially with colouring as the colours I prefer may not be the ones you do. The most important point is to relax and enjoy what you create as you wander down the garden path.

Alysa

Equipment and Techniques

Cold Porcelain

Cold porcelain is an air drying paste made from PVA glue, cornflower and baby oil - simple. All you need is a little muscle power to keep stirring when you are making it. Recipe Below.

Cold porcelain dries hard but is not brittle. If you roll the paste very fine, when dry there may be some flex which can add softness to the petals in the overall flower. Cold porcelain can shrink when dry. The recipe below has approx 5% shrinkage - some commercial pastes can shrink 15-20%. You will need to add white Arcrylic paint before use to prevent the paste drying opaque.

If you keep the cold porcelain wrapped in cling film and in an air tight container it will last. I find it better to make a small amount at a time - about 250 - 300g. You can use it straight away. Information regarding colouring is on page 8.

Ingredients • 1 of a good PVA glue • 1 cup good quality cornflour • 1 - 2 Tablespoons baby oil

Put the oil and glue in a NON-STICK saucepan and mix together with a wooden spoon. Stir in the cup of cornflour and mix it well in. Place over a low heat stirring constantly until like choux pastry it gathers around the spoon. It will get lumpy at first but keep going. When it rolls into a ball without sticking to your hands it's ready. Take off the heat and gently knead to clear any big lumps. Let it cool a little then rap in cling film and keep in an airtight container. You can use it straight away.

Tools

The photograph below shows all the tools and materials I have used to create the flowers within this book. The same tools, cutters and veiners that are used with Sugarcraft can be used with cold porcelain. It is surprising how many different effects can be achieved by using these tools in different ways. It is not always easy to explain in writing how to use the tools however. Perseverance is the key and coupled with practice comes knowledge.

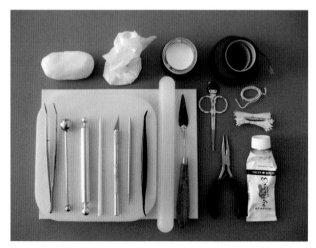

1. Cold Porcelain
2. Corn flour
3. PVA Glue
4. Floristry Tapes
5. Cel Board
6. Cel Pad
7. Surgical Tweezers
8. Ball Tool large
9. Ball Tool
10. Ceramic Veining Stick
11. Scalpel
12. Smooth cel stick
13 Jem Dresden/Veining tool
14. Rolling Pin
15. Palette Knife
16. Scissors
17. Pliers
18. Stamens
19. Embroidery Thread
20. White Acrylic Paint

Tools

The most useful tools for me are the ball tool, the ceramic silk veining tool, a pair of sharp nail scissors and surgical tweezers.

Use the ball tool to create softly curled petals and also to cup them.

For a gentle curl along the edge of a petal, place the ball half on and half off the edge of the paste and gently push forward with a smooth continuous motion around the whole shape. A gentle cupped effect is achieved by placing the ball tool just inside but away from the edge of the petal, and work as above. For deeply cupped petals, place the ball tool in the centre of the petal and make small circular motions which will curl up the sides. Use the ceramic cel stick to create varied textured finishes on the paste by rolling the tip or whole stick one way or back and forth. The tip can make an excellent ragged edge.

Cutters

I use both metal and plastic cutters however when working with cold porcelain I find metal cutters give a sharper cut. I have used KIT BOX Stainless Steel cutters throughout this book and worked closely with them to desgin a couple of extra ones for certain flowers. If paste is sticking to the cutter, rub a little cold cream around the edge before use, OR lightly dust cornflour onto the paste before cutting out. Keep your cutters clean - they will cut better and last longer.

Petal and Leaf Veiners

Cold Porcelain works well with both ceramic and rubber veiners. I have used mainly Squires Kitchen Great Impressions double sided veiners as they have an excellent range. Dust a little cornflour onto the ceramic veiner before use to avoid the paste sticking.

Wash veiners with warm soapy water before use to avoid transferring specs of colour onto clean paste. Red spots are my nemesis in this respect.

Florist tape

Gently pull the florist tape to release the gum whilst wrapping tightly down and around the stem. I have suggested widths of tape to use throughout, however use what you are comfortable with. The less tape for individual petals the better.

Wires

In general cut your wires longer rather than shorter as it is easier to cut them off than it is to add them on. I use white wires for petals and green for leaves. The lower the gauge number the thicker the wire.

Varnishing

To achieve a very high gloss shine, use full strength confectioner's varnish. Remove and spin the stem between your fingers and thumb to get rid of excess varnish.

For a softer shine mix equal quantities of confectioner's varnish with isopropanol alcohol (available from chemists) to get ½ strength varnish. You can also mix these two in ¼ and ¾ ratios (alcohol to varnish) to get varied 'shine' results., PME Edible Glaze - comes in a spray can, easy to use and gives a gloss finish.

Super Matt Sealing Spray from The Cromartie Group - comes in both gloss or matt finish. Hairspray is a good alternative as it also seals in the colour.

When using spray cans to varnish or for long periods of dusting with coloured powders, work in a ventilated area and wear a mask to avoid inhalation

Making leaves

Many leaves look similar in both shape, colour and veining. If you don't have a cutter and veiner for a particular flower, use leaf shapes such as rose, hydrangea and grapevine to give variety. It is amazing how you can change a leaf by colour and finish. Gloss and matt varnishing works wonders. In this book the main focus is on the flower and the foliage although important is not always critical in an arrangement - unless, of course, it is an exhibition piece!

Don't be afraid to take a leaf from the garden, cover with a little vaseline, place it over the paste and roll over the top to get the true vein impression.

COLOUR DUSTS

**SK - SQUIRES KITCHEN, SF - SUGARFLAIR, SM - THE SUGAR MILL
EA - EDIBLE ART, OP - ORCHARD PRODUCTS**

Forest Green SK, Leaf Green SK,
Spring Green SF and spring Green EA

Aubergine SF, Cyclamen SK,
Rose, SK, Red SF

Wild Poppy SM, Orangeade SM,
Tangerine SK and Tangy Tangerine SM

Dusky Pink SF, Pink SF,
Blackberry Shimmer EA and Plum SF

Autumn Gold SF, Hot Mustard SM,
Lemon SF and Primrose SF

Petal Blue SF, Bluebell SF,
Cornflower SF and Hydrangea SK

Iris EA, Lavender SF, Deep Purple SF
African Violet SF

Ivory SM, Cornish Cream SF
White SK, and Melon OP

Black SF, Nutkin Brown SF
Chocolate SF and Eucalyptus SF

C LOURING

The colours on the opposite page are there to give you a guide. There are many shades of each colour by different manufacturers and I have hardly ever used a single one on it's own! A good selection of brushes helps considerably and be bold in mixing your colours to get the result you want. For some flowers I have stated the colours used on the pages, but for others I have just advised shades of red, greens, blues etc.

Base Colours

Always add white acrylic paint to your porcelain before using. This prevents the porcelain appearing opaque when dry. Add base colour to your porcelain AFTER the white acrylic has been added. I have used the following paste colours within this book - Spruce Green (mid to dark green), Gooseberry (lime green) Dusky Pink, Grape Violet (purple), Cream, Tangerine and Melon (yellow).

Using colour dusts

1. Dust with colour when the cold porcelain is damp this way the colour will be absorbed into the paste as it dries.
2. Put a little dust onto a kitchen paper towel, dip in brush and tap off the excess to avoid applying too much at once.
3. In general dust from the bottom upwards to give a smooth even finish. Keep a couple of brushes to use to mix colours.
4. Experiment with colours. If you put darker colours on first, it will not be easy to lift the shade by adding lighter colours on top. Start with a lighter colour and you will have more control by adding depth and shading.
5. To make a paint, mix colour dust with a little water or clear alcohol (gin/vodka). Be careful not to make it too runny.
6. To make your own pollen, put some fine semolina into a small clear pot with a lid. Add in some colour dust and shake well. The depth of colour is controlled by the amount of colour dust used.
7. A selection of brushes of different widths and shapes is useful including very fine ones for painting.

Effects on leaves and petals

To reflect a 'crinkled edge' on your leaf, use a cel stick to roll firmly around the edge. Highlight the 'crinkle' with another colour, either lighter or darker than the main leaf.

To create a leaf to look like it has been nibbled or split, make a small cut through the front with a scalpel. Open it up slightly and dust around the edges of the split using a mix of dark green and aubergine.

Making a small tear along the edge of the leaf at an angle can be equally as effective and using different colours to highlight the tear gives another wonderful view of nature in it's true form.

Filler Flowers

No matter how well prepared I think I am, I often find myself looking for something to fill the gaps in arrangements! Sometimes it's just to add a bit of height, possibly to dangle down or just simply a hole to fill. With this in mind, I have included a selection of some of my favourite filler flowers that do the job with their varied shapes, each in their own delightful way.

Multiple Blossoms and mini Chrysanthemums

A very useful and versatile technique for making flowers in many sizes and shapes.

The Mini Chrysanthemums are striking with their bright lime green and equally effective are the blossoms - especially when the petals have been softened and curled. Sometimes I tape them into the neck of different larger flowers, nestled under the large petals. Even though they are not the same flower, in an arrangement they are not noticed as such and help to add good volume to the overall appearance.

Equipment
Ball tool, scalpel
Daisy cutters - KB - A005 (kitbox.co.uk)
Blossom cutters KB 005/006/007
Calyx cutter KB 005 (micro range)

Materials
White and pale green paste
28g wires
Nile green tape
Colours: spring green, tangerine, pink, plum and deep purple, cornflower & petal blue

Flowers - Blossoms and Chrysanthemums

1. Roll a tiny ball of white paste and insert at glued 28g white wire.

2. From white paste cut out petals from the 2 or 3 sizes of the chosen shape. The more petals you have the bigger the flower. You can vary the style of the flower by softening the edges of each sepal or by cutting down the centre of each one with a scalpel. If using the blossom cutter, cup each petal with a ball tool so the smaller petal will fit inside the larger one and so on.

3. Insert the tiny ball down through the centre of the smallest daisy/blossom petal. Glue around the ball and press the petals up against it leaving the tips rising above. Add on the others in the same way increasing in size as you go thereby creating an opening flower. Dust the flower whatever colour you like.

4. Using KB 005 cut out a flat calyx, or hat shaped calyx to suit the flower, insert the flower down through the centre and secure. Bend back the sepals of the calyx slightly to separate it from the flower. Dust with mid green and tape with ¼ width Nile green tape.

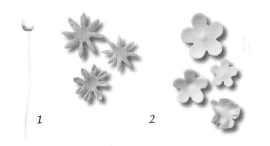

1   2

3   4

Leaves

To finish these flowers off, roll a small cone of green paste between your thumb and forefinger. Insert a 30g wire into the thick end and press the cone between thumb and finger into a small flat pointed leaf. Vein with a frilling tool and dust with shades of green. Make a selection of sizes - the bigger the cone the bigger the leaf.

Assembly

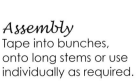

Tape into bunches, onto long stems or use individually as required.

13

Forget me not!

As children my sisters and I always included Forget me nots in the wild flowers we picked for our mother in an effort to get back into her good books!

Buds

1. Roll a small cone of white paste into the shape of a bud and attach it to a 28g wire. Roll another 4 buds of a similar size, shape, glue and gently attach them onto the side of the wired bud. Leave to dry a little and then dust with petal blue at the tip and spring green at the base.

2. Make individual larger wired buds in the same way as above. Gently indent the sides of some of the buds with scissors to represent petals. Dust as above.

Flowers

3, From a Mexican hat of white paste, cut out a blossom, ball around the edges of each petal. Insert a 28g white wire and push the arrow too into the centre of the blossom. Colour the centre yellow and dust soft blues around the outside. OR ...

4. Roll a very small and slim cone of white paste and insert a 28g wire. Flatten the tip and make a small hole in the centre. Dab a little glue over the top and dip into yellow pollen. Cut out a blossom as step 3, insert the centre down through the blossom and colour as before.

Equipment
Ball tool, arrow head tool
Blossom cutter KB 005

Materials
28g wire, Nile green tape
Yellow Pollen
Colours: yellow, cornflower, petal blue
light and mid green

Assembly

Tape into bunches or onto long stems as shown with ¼ width Nile green tape.

The Bride - Exochorda x macrantha

If you have seen this flower in full bloom you will know exactly why it is called The Bride. A waterfall of delicate white buds and blossoms packed along full stems cascading to the ground. Astoundingly beautiful it really takes your breath away by sheer unadulterated loveliness.

Half a dozen of these stems, the month of May, a Knight in shining armour .... perhaps, perhaps, perhaps!

Equipment
Ball tool, scissors, scalpel, ceramic veining tool
Apple Blossom KB A001
Blossom cutter KB 005

Materials
White & pale green paste
30 & 28g white and green wire
Nile green & dark brown florist tape
Pale green pollen
Colours: spring green, mid green chocolate dusts and lemon & autumn gold paint

15

Buds

1. Roll a selection of small balls ranging from 3 – 7mm dia. Glue and insert a 30g white wire. Tease a little of the paste down the stem. Flatten the top of the ball slightly and make a tiny snip with scissors on the paste at the bottom of the bud to give the impression of a calyx. Dust the very small buds completely with light green.

2. For the larger buds, with a veining tool or scalpel make a couple of indentations around the sides of the bud. Dust the base and the snipped calyx with light green, leaving the rest of the bud mainly white. Tape stems with ¼ width Nile green tape.

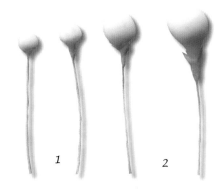

Flowers

3. Make a small ball 3mm dia. Glue and insert a 30g white wire. Rough up the top of the ball with a scalpel and dip into pale green pollen.

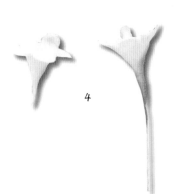

4. Roll a Mexican hat of white paste, cut out a 5 petal blossom, soften each of the petals and cup slightly. Insert the ball down through the centre of the blossom until it is tucked into the hollow and secure neatly to the stem. Allow to dry a little.

5. Cut out 5 fine white petals with the A001 cutter, soften the edges, vein and shape. Turn the blossom upside down and attach each petal to the back in between the blossom petals with a little glue. Let the new petals rest in position for the glue to dry and then turn over and gently shape them with your fingers by pinching, curling and cupping to give movement. Vary the openness of the flower by cupping the petals from tight to open positions. Leave a petal off here and there to age the flower for variety. Allow to dry.

6. Paint around the centre of the flower with a circle of yellow/green dust paint. Finely dot specks of light brown paint around the centre to simulate stamens. Tape the stems with ¼ width Nile green tape.

6

7　　　　　　　*8*

Seed Pods - 3 stages

7. Roll a small ball of green or brown paste. Insert a glued 30g wire and squash almost flat between your fingers. Dust with dark brown and leave to dry.

8. Roll a slightly larger ball of paste into an oval. Insert a glued 30g wire. Using your fingers or tweezers pinch out 3 sides. Dust with dark brown over green and leave to dry.

9. Roll 3 small balls of brown paste the same size. Squash each ball into a flat circle between your fingers and thumb. Make a crease down the centre and fold in two but don't let the sides stick together. Dust dark brown. Dab a little glue along the folded edge of each and stick together. Glue and insert a 30g green wire through the centre. Leave to dry.

10. Tape these buds into a stem, with ¼ width dark brown tape varying the stages of the buds along the way.

9

10

Leaves

Roll a small oblong of pale green paste, insert a 30g wire and squash between your fingers into a thin oval shaped leaf. Pinch the base of the leaf at the join of the stem to secure. Vein down the centre with a veining tool, shape and dust with light and mid green. Make several difference sizes. Tape these leaves in amongst the buds and flowers.

17

Assembly

Tape the buds and flowers into individual stems at various intervals. Use their own wire stems until you need to add a 24g wire for strength. The buds and the flowers open at different places on the stem, so there is no need to have just the buds or the flowers at the top. Use ¼ width Nile green tape.

Tape the stems together onto a 22g wire keeping a leading stem and bring the others in from the sides as you move down.

WILD MARSH FLOWERS

This is a joy of a flower to make. I have no idea what it is called but I found it in the marsh when walking with my dog, Beth. Swaying in the breeze with a smile on it's face it is stunning in simplicity and can be adapted in colour to suit whatever the theme. Pale and interesting or dark and dramatic - the options are endless!

Equipment
Ball tool and scalpel
Ceramic veining tool
Apple blossom cutter KB A001
Pansy veiner SK GI

Materials
White paste
Cream embroidery thread
33 & 28g white wire
Nile green florist tape
Colours: dusky pink, iris, lavender,
spring green & primrose
Brown/rusty paint

Buds

1. Roll 3 tiny teardrops of white paste. Dab a little glue onto one side of each at the thick end and stick to each other. Insert a glued 30g white wire up through the middle of the group and press gently together to secure. Dust the bottom with light green and the top with shades of Iris and Lavender. Make 2 or 3 of these groups, varying the number of little buds between 3 and 5.

2. Roll more teardrops of sizes 5 - 7mm in length. With sharp scissors, snip little cuts around the bottom of each to act as a calyx. Glue and insert a 30g wire. Dust the snips for the calyx in light green and the rest of the bud as before. Make the bigger buds slightly more round at the top as if they are opening up.

3. Dust the white stems with light green and tape together into groups of 9 - 12 onto a 28g wire using ¼ width Nile green tape.

1 *2* *3*

Flower Stamens

4. Cut the embroidery thread into 2cm lengths. Tape it onto a 28g wire leaving 1cm showing at the top. Separate the 6 individual threads and dust with light green. Paint the tips with brown paint.

Petals

5. Roll out some thin white paste and cut out 4 petals. Insert a 33g white wire. Tease the paste slightly down the wire. Soften the edge and vein. Dust the bottom of the petal with a mix of pale yellow and light green and the rest of the petal with lilac.

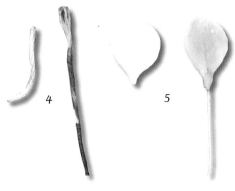

4 *5*

6. Tape 4 petals tightly around the base of the stamen with ¼ width Nile green tape. Make 4 flowers.

6

Assembly
Tape 4 flowers around a central group of buds keeping them equal in height. Tape down the stem with ¼ width Nile green tape.

If you want some leaves to go with these, make them in the same way as for Golden Rod on p68

21

BERBERRIS Vulgaris

Languishing in the shade of the Beech Hedge, sits a Berberris. My son Peter chose this as a memorial plant for his pet Gecko, Greg. He said that as a colourful and constantly changing shrub it reminded him of his friend.

In Spring it ignites with clusters of bright orange buds and blossoms amid a dark green foliage. After the petals fall from the flowers, for Summer we are privy to a display of berries of changing colours. First they appear as a mass of striking green with burgundy stems ripening to a rich and velvety purple as Autumn approaches.

With this range of colour, it is perfect for filling in.

The Berries are rich in Vitamin C and quite bitter, but be warned - the rest of the plant is mildly poisonous!

Materials
White, purple and pale green paste
30 & 24g green wire
33g white wire
Red and twig floristry tape
Colours: a mix of oranges, purples greens and red

Equipment
Ball tool, scalpel
Berberris cutter KB 0435
Berberris leaf cutter KB A015
Holly leaf veiner SKG1

Spring Buds

1. Roll lots of small balls of white paste ranging in sizes up to the size of a small pea. Glue and insert a 33g white wire.

2. With scissors or a scalpel make indentations on the sides of the buds to mimic unopened petals. Dust with rich orange and a touch of red at the base.

3. Paint the wire of the bud with red colour dust mixed with a little water.

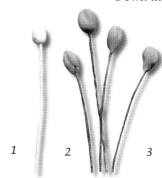

Flowers

4. Roll out some white paste and cut out 2 of the small size blossom petals, soften and dust with rich orange.

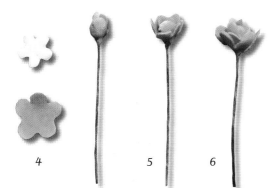

5. Dab a little glue around a very small bud and insert the stem down through the centre of a blossom. Squeeze together the petals around the ball. Repeat with the second blossom petal leaving it a little more open. Make flowers of different sizes by adding 1, 2 or 3 petals as shown.

6. Cut out a final petal with the larger cutter, soften and add to the flower, again leaving it more open. Dust the bottom of the flower with a little red.

Add a touch of variety and make these berries - always a treat!

Summer Berries

7. Use pale green paste and roll some small oval berries. Insert a 33g white wire through the berry so it just peeps out of the top. Dust the berry with bright green with a touch of red at the base of the berry and paint the wire red.

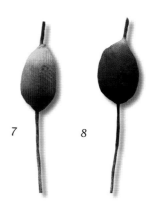

Autumn Berries

8. Use purple paste and repeat the steps as for Summer berries but make the ovals larger to look plump and juicy. Dust with a deep purple mixed with dark blue.

23

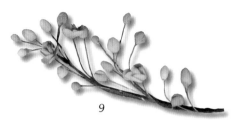

9. Tape with ¼ width red tape into small groups of buds and flowers. Attach the groups of berries onto a 26g wire still using the ¼ width red tape as shown. Small bracts appear on the stem, so make these by snipping a little of the tape, pull it away from the stem and dust the tip with yellow.

9

Leaves

Use 28g wire and leaf cutter A015 to make some leaves . Vein with the SKGI Holly veiner and colour dark green dusting the very tips of the spikes with yellow.

Assembly

Tape a bunch of buds and flowers to 24g wire using twig tape. Add in leaves and other bunches of flowers at intervals down the stem. Make additional branches of flowers to add in along the way.

Cold porcelain Berberis and leaves placed with the real shrub in the garden

SILVER BIRCH - CATKINS

It is a definite sign of Spring when the catkins appear.

My mother used to call them lamb's tails and I recall as a child picking them off the tree, dropping them around the kitchen and telling anyone who would listen that we had been invaded by caterpillars!

Quick and easy they are extremely effective and definitely a great talking point.

Equipment
Ball tool, scissors
Rose/Silver Birch leaf cutter KB 039-041
Tea Rose leaf veiner - small SKGI

Materials
Pale green and cream paste
30, 28 & 24g green wire
Nile green and twig tape
Colours: mid to light greens, yellow, cream and brown paint

Catkins

1. Roll a thin sausage of cream paste 1.5 - 2cm long. Glue and insert a 30g wire.

2. With scissors, snip V cuts around the length of the catkin all the way down. Dust with a mix of pale yellow and cream. Paint the tips of the points of the snips with brown. Tape the stem with ¼ width twig tape.

1   *2*

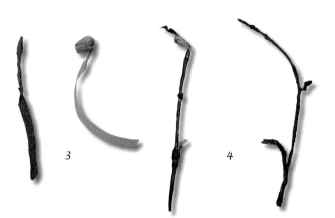

3   *4*

Twigs

3. Twist back on itself some ¼ width twig tape to make into a brown bud at the tip of the stem and tape onto a 28g wire. Roll ¼ width Nile green tape in the same way a little larger to resemble a budding leaf.

4. Attach it onto the main stem with the ¼ width twig tape. Make a couple of these buds in various sizes as you move down the stem.

Leaves

5. From pale green paste, cut out a selection of leaves in various sizes. Glue and insert a 30g wire, soften the edges, vein and colour with fresh light green and yellow dusts. Edge some leaves with brown. Make a small hole in a couple of the leaves and paint around the inside edge with chestnut. Shape and leave to dry. Tape stem with ¼ width Nile green tape.

6. Loosely twist with your fingers 2cm of full width tape and fold the tip back over so it looks like a crinkled leaf just opening up. Tape to the twig in between two leaves with ¼ width twig tape.

5

7

6

7. Add a catkin or two at the top of a 28g wire with ¼ width twig tape and continue down the stem as step 4 adding in buds, leaves and more catkins.

Assembly
Tape the individual stems together into small branches, taping in stronger wire as required to support the weight. Remember the branches appear light and delicate so make sure that they are not too solid and keep their movement.

GRAPE HYACINTH

These gems seem to pop up all over the place!

With their tall upright stems rising from rather floppy long green leaves, they stand to attention in the flower bed making sure you can't miss them with their vibrant blue to purple urn shaped tightly packed flowers tipped with white frills.

Great for height in an arrangement but also can be cut short to fill a gap.

Equipment
Scissors, cocktail stick
Tulip Leaf veiner SKGI

Materials
White paste
33 & 24g white wire
Medium seed head stamens cut in half
Nile green florist tape
Colours: cornflower, petal blue and a touch of purple to mix.

Buds

1. Roll a dozen tiny to small ovals of white paste. Glue and insert a 33g wire. Make a small hole in the slightly larger ones with a cocktail stick and gently impress a couple of indents on the outside with scissors.

2. Dust lightly with petal and cornflower blue.

Opening buds to flowers

3. Roll approx. 30 teardrops of white paste in varying sizes – max 5-6mm long. Insert one blade of the scissors into the thicker end and snip around the very tip of the sides of the ball to make little petals. Insert a seed head stamen down through the centre and secure.

4. Starting from the stem, dust with darker shades of blue and purple leaving the tips of the opening petals white.

Leaves

Cut out freehand some long slender leaves from green paste. Glue and insert a 26g wire, about 1". Soften the edges and vein with the tulip leaf veiner. These leaves are quite floppy in real life, however to make better use of them in an arrangement leave to dry with just a gentle curl.

Assembly

Tape the smallest buds to the top and around a 22g wire with ¼ width Nile green tape. Add in the larger buds to the stem creating a tightly packed or more open shape. The stems of these lovely flowers are quite thick so build it up with ½ width tape as you go down.

MAIN FLOWERS

I have chosen the flowers that follow not only because they conjure up the essence of a country garden, but also for the varied techniques used to make them. With these skills, together with the ones used to make the filler flowers, you will be able to adapt them to suit many other flowers that you would like to re-create in cold porcelain.

SWEET PEA

As a charming old fashioned flower, Sweet peas captivate an audience with their colourful display and enticing fragrance. Like bees to a honey pot, I challenge anyone to walk past without saying …..
mmmmm … lovely!

They are wonderful as cut flowers light and delicate bringing tranquillity and harmony to any room. Their image automatically creates a fragrance and therefore perfect to make in cold porcelain.

I usually make all my sweet peas in white to be able to vary the colours with dusts or by airbrushing. However, experiment by using pastel colours as a base to create depth and deeper shades of colour.

Equipment
Ball tool
Sweet Pea cutter KB A013
Small calyx cutter KB A002

Materials
White porcelain paste
28g white wire
30g green wire
Nile green floristry tape
Colours: pinks, purples, greens and yellow

Centres

1. Roll a large pea sized ball of white paste. Squash between your fingers and thumb into a flat oval.

2. Place a hooked 28g white wire into the middle of the oval, fold the oval in half and gently pinch the edges to secure. Dust lightly with pale yellow and green.

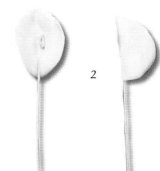

Petals

3. Cut out an inside petal from white paste. Soften by rolling around the edges with a cell stick to create a gentle frill.

4. Glue down the back of the seedpod and place onto the inside petal. Secure leaving the petals open at the front.

5. Cut an outer petal and soften the edges with a ball tool - not quite so frilled as the inside petal.

6. Glue down the back edge of the inside petal and secure the outer petal as before letting the petal bend back slightly.

7. From a green Mexican hat cut out a small calyx, glue and insert the stem of the flower down through the centre and secure. Dust the calyx with medium to light green.

8. Lightly dust the edges of the centre petal with your preferred colour and more deeply at the base of the back petal brushing up towards the top.

Tendrils

To add interest make some tendrils by winding a 30g green wire or twisted ¼ width Nile green tape around a cel stick and tape to the stem of a flower.

A Bridesmaid's posy ball of cold porcelain Sweet peas complete with a set of freshwater pearls as a handle.

HYDRANGEA - MOP HEAD

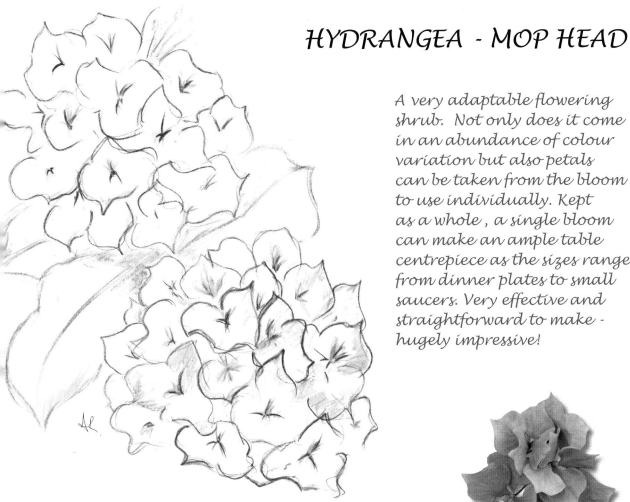

A very adaptable flowering shrub. Not only does it come in an abundance of colour variation but also petals can be taken from the bloom to use individually. Kept as a whole, a single bloom can make an ample table centrepiece as the sizes range from dinner plates to small saucers. Very effective and straightforward to make - hugely impressive!

Equipment
Hydrangea petal cutter KB A009
Hydrangea leaf cutter KB A018
Hydrangea petal veiner SKGI
Hydrangea leaf veiner SKGI
Tweezers

Materials
White & green porcelain paste
30g white wire cut into 4
26 & 20g green wire
Nile green florist tape
Colours: A mix of hydrangea, cornflower and petal blue, pinks and African violet

Central pip

1. Roll a 4mm ball of white paste. Cut a 30g wire into 4. Insert a glued wire and tease the paste slightly down the stem leaving a ball at the top. With tweezers pinch small segments of paste around the ball 3 or 4 times making ridges. Dust with the colour of your chosen flowers.

Flowers

2. Roll out fine white paste and cut out 4 petals per individual flower. Insert a 30g glued wire, soften the edges and vein. Dust from the bottom to the top with your chosen colour.

3. Tape 4 petals tightly around the base of a central pip with ¼ width Nile green tape. Do this before the petals are completely dry so they will form well against each other.

1

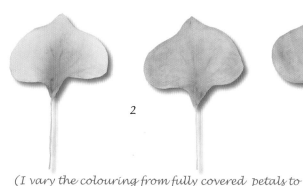

2

3

(I vary the colouring from fully covered petals to dark at the bottom and lighter at the top)

4. Tape a single flower onto the top of a 20g wire. Add on the other flowers, tucking them closely together but also allowing movement of the petals. Try and keep a ball shape. This can be between 12 to 15 individual sets of 4 petals i.e. 15 x 4 = 60 individual petals for a large flower.

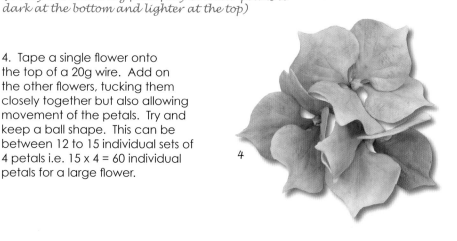

4

Leaves

Cut a 26g wire into 6. Roll out some green porcelain and cut out several leaves. Insert a glued wire, soften the edges and vein. Colour with medium rich greens, and dust around the edges with burgundy to highlight. Shape and leave to dry. Varnish with a ¼ glaze confectioners varnish.

To add interest, make a group of central pips, or using a mini calyx cutter individual flowers using a Mexican hat method. Tape into groups and insert into the overall bloom to break it up.

Assembly

Use full width Nile green tape to add thickness to the stem and add in the leaves. There are two smaller leaves directly under the flower, followed by larger leaves set in pairs as they go down the stem. Paint small flecks of red onto the main stem of tape.

HYDRANGEA - PETIOLARIS

This robust climbing shrub covers the east facing gable of my home. A mass of impressive vibrant green foliage dotted through with delicate white lacy flowers, it is a welcoming sight when I arrive back from a long journey.

Takes a little time to make, but well worth the effort. The flowers display themselves beautifully without the need for leaves. I make the buds the same way I do blackberry pips - either at night with a gin and tonic infront of the telly or during the day as an excuse to grab a moments sunshine in the garden !

Equipment
Apple Blossom Cutters KB 0053
Ball tool

Materials
While and pale green porcelain
33g white & 24g green wire
Nile green tape
Colours: spring & leaf green, primrose

Centre buds

1. Cut a 33g green wire into 6. Roll a small ball of pale green paste, insert a glued wire up through the ball so it is just peeping through the top. Pinch the paste up around the extended wire. Dust with a mix of Spring and leaf green. Make 100 - 150 of these. Tape together into groups of varied numbers from 3 - 9 with ¼ width Nile green tape. Make 1 large group of 15 buds and attach to a 22g wire. Keep this separate for the assembly.

Flowers

2. Cut a 30g white wire into 4. Roll a very small ball of white paste and insert a glued wire. Dust softly with yellow and light green.

3. Roll out fine white paste. Cut out 4 petals per flower. Glue and insert a 33g white wire into each petal, soften the edges on your hand, using your thumb to give a light veining. Cup slightly, dust very lightly at the bottom to match the pip and leave to dry.

4. Tape each petal tightly to the base evenly around the pip.

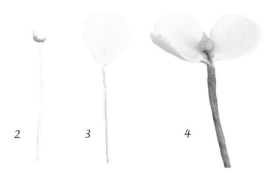

5. Tape a small group of buds 3 cm down the stem of a flower adding a slightly larger group 2 cms below. Bend them upwards away from the stem. The aim is to keep the buds roughly at the same height no matter where you have taped them on the stem. Add 3 - 5 groups of buds on each stem.

Assembly

Attach the 5 petal stems onto the prepared centre stem, underneath the large group of buds. Bend the wires to keep the overall arrangement flat. Dust over the main stem with rusty browns. The buds all merge together making a central feature while the flowers surround them on the outside.

As the flowers fade they turn a beautiful shade of lime green then to soft brown.

Cold porcelain Petiolaris placed in the real shrub

APPLE BLOSSOM

In the middle of my garden is a very old Apple Tree loved by all the family - espcially Felix who is often seen hanging from a branch!

Every Spring, without fail, this true friend offers a display of pure beauty totally without condition. The grass beneath is carpeted with blossom and although the petals will fall, they are replaced by the sweetest apples. When the Winter sets in and the days are dark, it warms my heart to know that in just a few months it will all bloom again.

Until then I will capture it in porcelain.

Equipment
Ball tool, tweezers
Calyx cutter KB A002
Small Rose / Apple Blossom petal cutter KB0053
Metal leaf cutters KB A019
Apple Tree Leaf Veiner SKGI

Materials
White and pale green paste
Small stamens (Norma's Noblies)
30, 28, 26 & 20g wires
Nile green and twig florist tape
Pale yellow pollen
Colours: plum, pink, greens and brown

Buds

1. Roll a small pea size ball of white paste and insert a 30g wire.

2. Cut out 3 small petals and soften the edges. Glue and wrap the first petal around the ball leaving an open edge. Insert the second petal in between the open edge of the first petal and the ball and wrap around. Continue with the third petal in the same way and secure. Make sure that the petals interlink and rise above the top of the ball. Tape the stem with ¼ width Nile green tape.

3. Cut out a calyx from green paste. Soften the edges and dust lightly with shades of green. Insert the stem of the bud down through the top of the calyx and secure. Dust the edges of the petals with shades of pink.

For a tightly closed bud, colour more deeply and vary the size of petal to create smaller and larger buds

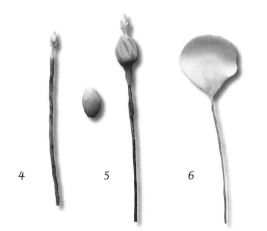

Blossoms

4. Tape 3 small stamens onto a 30g wire. Dab a little glue onto the stamens and dip into the pollen.

5. Roll a small oval of green paste and insert the stamens down through the ball until the tips of the stamens are showing. Pinch to secure and dust with light green. Use tweezers to pinch grooves around the centre ball.

6. Cut out 5 white petals and insert a 33g wire. Soften the edges and vein on your hand. Dust the edges with shades of pink.

7. Gently bend the wire at the base of the petal, tuck neatly under the stamen ball and tape with ¼ width Nile green tape. Tape the other 4 petals around the stamen in the same way.

8. Cut out and colour a calyx as before, insert the flower stem down through the top and secure.   Finish off by adding a little more colour to the back of the petals as required.

7

8

9. Tape the flowers and buds together in groups of 3 & 5 with ½ width Nile green florist tape. Dust the tape with a little soft brown so to blend with the main stem when assembled.

9

Leaves

Cut out leaves in various sizes, vein and colour mixing shades of green, yellow and brown. Lighter shades for the younger leaves. Edge the older ones with a touch of brown. Tape stems 1cm with ¼ width Nile green tape.

Assembly

Group the blossoms together mixing buds and flowers. Use twig tape to overlap the top of a 24g wire to make a leading bud. Add in the smaller leaves first moving down the branch to include clusters of flowers where you see fit. Tape in a 20g wire when the branch needs more strength..

CLEMATIS
EARLY SENSATION

Rightly named 'Early Sensation' this clematis is a lovely example of Spring blooms. It climbs up the wall and around the back door in a fairly sheltered position. I planted it in a large pot in the hope of having some control over the growth, however this evergreen climber with it's bright white flowers, vibrant yellow centres and 'designer' leaves has a mind of it's own.

Equipment
Ball tool, scissors, scalpel,
Ceramic veining tool
8 petal narrow Daisy cutter KB A005
Clematis petal cutter KB A004
Clematis Montana petal veiner SKGI
Clematis leaf cutter KB A016

Materials
White and pale green paste
28, 28 & 22g green wire
30g white wire
Nile green and twig floristry tape
Colours: primrose, lemon, mixed greens and brown. Brown paint.

Buds

1. Roll a cone of white paste 1.5 cm in length. Hook, glue and insert a 28g white wire. Using a scalpel or frilling tool to mark 3 or 4 lines from the top of the bud to the base. Tape down the stem 2 cm with Nile green tape. Dust with a little light green at the base. To vary the buds, use sharp scissors to snip the very top into 4 as if the petals are just about to open. Make 6 or 7 buds at different stages as they are fantastic fillers.

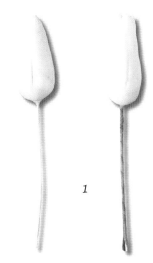

1

2

2. For an opening bud, use the petal cutter A004 and cut out 7 petals from white paste. Insert a 28g wire , soften, vein and lightly ripple the edges of each petal curling them in towards each other. Dust the base of the petals with light green then tape the stems tightly together with ¼ width Nile green tape.

Flower Centre - stamens

3. Roll a tiny ball of white paste and insert at glued 28g white wire.

4. From yellow paste cut out 3 flat 8 petal small daisies and 1 larger. Cut down the centre of each of the sepals with a scalpel.

5. Insert the tiny ball down through the first daisy and glue the blossom around the ball leaving the tips rising above. Add on the other two in the same way, creating an opening centre. Add on the larger daisy onto the stem, secure with a little glue but let it stay open. Dust the centre with a mix of pale yellow and green. Paint the tips of the bottom layer with brown paint. See Step 7 photo.

3   4   5

Petals

6. From white paste cut out 6 petals. Insert a 28g white wire, soften the edges and vein. These petals are pure white, so depending on how clean your paste is, if required you can over dust with a little white adding a tiny touch of light green just at the base of the petal to keep it looking fresh.

7. Tape the petals tightly around the base of the flower centre securing with ¼ width Nile green florist tape.

6

7

Leaves

Using the template or cutters, make a selection of leaves using 26g green wire. Vein by hand using the Jem veining tool and dust with shades of green. Paint along the edge of some of the leaves with brown. Tape 2cm down the stem with ¼ width twig tape. Varnish with matt sealing spray and tape into sets of 2 or 3 leaves.

Assembly

Starting with a set of leaves at the top, tape onto a 24g wire with twig tape, adding a couple of buds and a group of flowers interspersed with leaves as you carry on down the stem. Make a separate branch of flowers to join onto the main stem building your spray to whatever length you need.

Using the same techniques, experiment with petals of different sizes and coloured centres to create your own species of Clematis.

A piece of driftwood found on the beach gives an opportunity to display a branch of clematis in a natural way making a very attractive table centrepiece.

HIMALAYAN BLUE POPPY - Meconopsis sp

A reflection of all the blues in the sky, this tall perennial plant stands almost 4ft high on relatively thin but obviously strong stems.

Originating from the cool mountainous regions of Tibet this Himalayan Blue Poppy requires a cool sheltered position. Five years ago it appeared in the garden - I know not how - but certainly chose the right spot next to the purple delphiniums and has spread considerably offering an abundance of magical blue flowers throughout July and August.

Equipment
Ball tool, tweezers, veining tool
Rose Petal Cutter KB 0519
Peony petal veiner SKGI
Primrose leaf veiner SKGI

Materials
White and pale green paste
Dried gypsophila
28, 26 & 18g white wire
Yellow & brown pollen
Nile green florist tape
Colours: bluebell, cornflower, African violet, mid green and eucalyptus.

Buds - closed

1. Roll a plump slightly oval cone of pale green paste approx 1.5cm in length. Glue and insert a 26g wire. Mark two lines on either side from tip to base of the cone to identify the sepals. These sepals are protecting the petals inside. Dust with soft mid green and eucalyptus. Scrape the cone/sepals with a cocktail stick to rough up the outside. Dust lightly over the raised rough tips with a mix of pale yellow and brown to make them stand out. When dry, paint a little glue over the surface and sprinkle with light brown pollen.

1

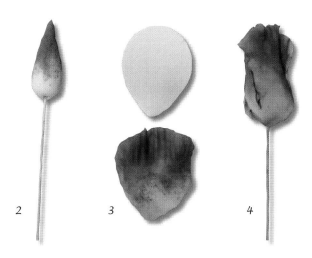

2   *3*   *4*

Buds - opening

2. Make a small slender cone of white paste. Glue and insert a 28g wire. Dust pale blue.

3. Cut out 2 petals with the smallest cutter. Soften the edges, frill the top edge and dust with a deep blue.

4. Glue the cone and wrap the first petal tightly around the bud, overlapping the top. Put a touch of glue on the 2nd petal and wrap around the 1st, keeping it a little more open, and leave to dry.

5. Cut out two ovals of green paste slightly shorter than the length of the petals of the bud. Dust with soft mid green and eucalyptus.

6. Place a little glue on the base of each sepal and secure to the base of the petal bud joining together at the sides and leaving the top open. Scrape the sepals with a cocktail stick to rough up the outside. Dust lightly over the raised rough tips with a mix of pale yellow and brown to make them stand out.

7. Use the paste at the base of the sepal to create a small hip blending into the stem. Tape the stem with ½ width Nile green tape and dust the tape with some eucalyptus to match in with the sepals. When dry paint a weak glue over the sepals and sprinkle very lightly with light brown pollen.

5

6 & 7

Flowers - Pistol

8. Take a ball of white paste about 7mm in diameter, glue and insert a 28g wire. Tease the paste down the wire 2cm leaving a ball at the top and a slightly rounded area at the bottom.

9. With tweezers, pinch out 4 equal sections around the top of the pistol. Make a small indent with a scalpel along the centre of each section. This is the stigma. Dust pale green and then around the top with nutkin brown.

10. Cut a bunch of dried gypsophila to make the stamens. Dampen it slightly and dip into a rich yellow pollen. Tape the stamens around the base of the pistol with ¼ width Nile green tape.

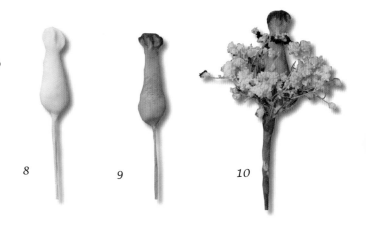

8   9   10

11   12

A cardboard fruit tray from a supermarket is an excellent mould to help form petals as they dry.

Petals

11. Cut out 4 petals from white paste using the medium or large cutter. Glue and insert a 28g white wire. Soften the edges and vein. Use a frilling tool to ripple the top edges and spread the petal. Cup the base of the petal, shape and leave to dry. Tape the wire with ¼ width Nile green tape.

12. Secure the petals tightly to the base of the stamens with ½ width Nile green tape. Use the tape to thicken the main stem and dust over with a little eucalyptus.

Leaves

I have used the rose petal cutters with a primrose leaf veiner for these leaves and just stretched them in length. Use 28g wire and colour with mid greens and cover with eucalyptus. This leaf is matt in appearance.

Assembly

Tape a flower and bud onto a 20g wire with Nile green tape. Add a group of leaves just below the bud. These are very tall plants with long stems with poppies forming all the way up the stem at various intervals.

DOUBLE RED POPPY

I so look forward to May when both sides of the path are a blaze of orange and red. These fabulous enormous poppies just keep coming and coming - almost overwhelming the flower beds. With petals wafer thin like butterfly wings they bring warmth and colour after the daffodils have gone. They have long and straggly stems so work as a team, holding each other up in their masses.

The dried seed pods make wonderful Christmas decorations when sprayed gold or silver and pushed into an oasis.

Equipment
Ball tool, tweezers
Ceramic ceining tool
Poppy cutters KB A012
Poppy Petals Veiner SKGI

Materials
Green and pale orange porcelain
Norma's noblies stamens large
28, 24 & 18g wire
Colours: wild poppy, aubergine, reds,
oranges and greens. Brown paint

Poppy Centre

1. Roll an oval of green paste, about 2.5cm long and 1cm wide. Put your first two fingers and thumb together and push down on the top to make the tip into a cone.

2. Glue and insert a hooked 18g wire pinching off any excess paste and secure. With a pair of tweezers - surgical ones are good for this - pinch from the top of the cone down to the ridge 7 times. Dust the ridges with a mix of aubergine and purple and the main trunk darker green.

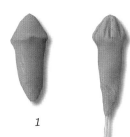 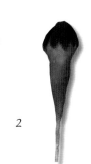

1   *2*

3

Stamens

3. Take a large group of stamens, enough to go around the poppy centre. Paint their heads brown by mixing petal dust with water. Tape the stamens equally around the centre keeping the tip showing.

Petals

Poppy petals are wafer thin. Not always easy to achieve, but the finer you can roll the paste the more effective the flower becomes. There are 3 sizes of petals used for this poppy. They are all made in the same way.

4. Cut out 9 small petals. Insert a 28g wire, soften and widen slightly with the ball tool. Vein with either the poppy veiner or the ceramic veining tool and ripple across the top edge. Dust with wild poppy and a touch of orange.

5. Repeat step 3 using the medium petal. Make at lease 9 petals.

6. Repeat step 3 using the largest petal. Make 12 petals.

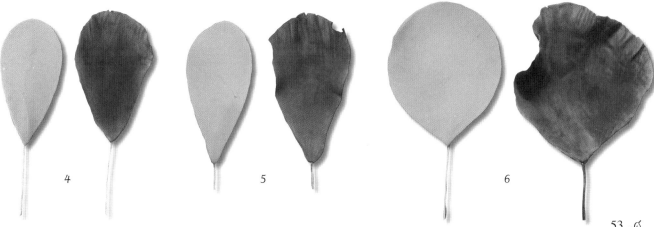

4   *5*   *6*

Assembly

Tape the petals around the centre with Nile green tape starting with the smallest. Tape all the petals to the stem when they are firm but not dry. This way they still have flexibility and will fit in against each other. Tape down the stem with full width tape to make a thick stem.

A double headed poppy beside the garden path

PHILADELPHUS - 'Snowbelle'

An eruption of fragrance hits you in the early evening as you walk past this compact deciduous shrub. Covered in clusters of pure white flowers and surrounded by neat rich green leaves, it really is a show stopper. Thought I'd done some damage with a hefty prune last Autumn, but thankfully it seemed to have enjoyed the haircut and is thriving this year.

Equipment
Ball tool
Ceramic veining tool
Rose petal cutters KB 0052
Small Metal leaf/petal cutters KB A09
Small & med Calyx cutter KB A002
Rose petal or small Lily veiner SKGI
Multi- leaf veiner - or fresh leaf

Materials
White & green porcelain paste
28 & 30g white & green wire
Dark green florist tape.
Colours: range of greens and light yellow

Buds

1. Roll a 1cm long fat cone from white paste. Glue and insert a 28g wire.

2. Roll fine white paste and cut out 3 small rose petals. Using a cel stick, vein and spread each petal by placing the stick point down the centre of the petal and gently roll from side to side.

3. Glue the cone and place the petals around it covering the tip and interlocking with each other to cover the cone completely.

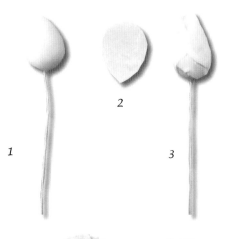

4. Make a Mexican hat and cut out a small green calyx. Soften the edges of the sepals. Glue the centre of the calyx and attach to the bottom of the cone. Dust the calyx with mid green.

5. Make larger buds by simply adding more layers of petals around the cone. Increase the size of petals as the buds get larger. Finish with a calyx in the same way as step 4.

Flowers

6. Twist a length of ¼ width white tape. Bend it into two hoops and attach to a 28g wire. Roll a small pip and insert the stamens down through the top. Cut the hoops and dust the stamens and the hip pale yellow.

7. Roll out fine white paste and cut 7 petals with the small pointed metal leaf/petal cutter. Soften in your hands, glue the base of the petal and attach to the bottom of the pip. Continue adding petals around the stamen, overlapping the previous petal as you go.

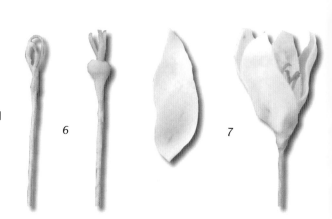

8. Roll out slightly thicker white paste, using the same cutter and cut out another 7 petals. Using your hands or a ball tool soften and slightly stretch out the petal sides - making them a little larger than the first set. Attach in the same way, but try not to make the base too bulky. Cup the flower to keep it rounded

Wired Petals

9. Using a rose petal cutter of a suitable size, cut out 5 petals. Glue and insert a 28g wire, soften the edges and vein with a rose petal or the lily veiner. Roll the edges with a cel stick to get movement, cup slightly and leave to dry. When firm but flexible, attach to the flower with ¼ Nile green tape just under the bowl of the flower.

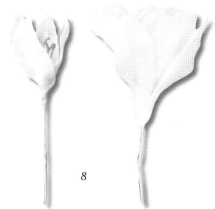

8

10. Add a calyx to suit the size of your flower. Smooth into the neck of the stem as much as possible and colour with green.

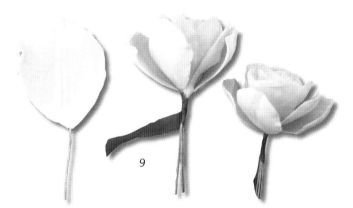

9

10

Leaves

Make a mix of sizes of leaves with your chosen cutter and veiner. Dust with rich green, darker in the middle with a touch of yellow on the outer leaf.

I used the hydrangea leaf cutter and took a leaf from the garden. Coat the underside of the leaf with a thin layer of Vaseline so it will not stick, lay the leaf on top of the paste and gently roll over to get an impression of the veining,

Assembly

Tape all individual stems with ¼ width Nile green tape. Group together a couple of flowers and tape onto a 20g wire. Add in two small leaves underneath the flowers. Move down the stem about an inch and add in another set of flowers and buds. Tape in larger leaves the further you go down the branch.

WALLFLOWERS

A pretty and colourful plant which just makes you smile when you see it. Like the Sweet Pea I cannot walk past without stopping and to have a sniff! With colours ranging from shades of red to orange and yellow in many combinations, it truly adds character to arrangements and is definitely one of my favourites!

Equipment
Ball tool, Ceramic veining tool
Scissors
Wallflower petal & calyx cutter KB A014
Pansy petal veiner SKGI
Narrow leaf cutters KB A020

Materials
White & green porcelain paste
Tiny seed head stamens (yellow)
28 & 20g green wire
28, 30 white wire
Nile green floristy tape
Colours: reds, yellow, orange & greens

Buds

1. Roll a small cone of white paste into the shape of a bud and attach it to a 30g wire. Roll another 4 buds of a similar size and shape, glue and gently attach them onto the side of the wired bud. Leave to dry a little and then dust with dark aubergine and burgundy.

2. Make individual larger wired buds in the same way as above. Gently indent the sides with scissors to represent petals. Colour to match the small group.

3. Roll out 2 petals from thin white paste, soften the edges, vein and colour as buds. Glue over a larger bud and wrap the two petals tightly around, leaving the top a little open. Cut out a flat calyx, dust to match and attach to the bud.

4. Tape a group of buds together with the smallest in the centre and the larger ones towards the outside.

Flowers

5. Tape 5 small stamens to a 30g wire with ¼ width Nile green tape, dust pale yellow.

6. Cut out 4 petals from white paste. Glue and insert a 30g white wire. Stretch the paste slightly down the wire. Soften the edges and vein with the Pansy petal veiner.

7. For burgundy flowers dust a little yellow at the base of the petal and continue upwards with a mix of burgundy and aubergine. Dust the same on the back.

For yellow flowers, use a strong bright yellow and dust the whole petal. You can vary your yellow flowers by lightly brushing over some of the petals with burgundy.

When coloured, cup 2 petals backwards and 2 forwards. Leave to dry.

8. Tape the petals tightly around the base of the stamen with ¼ width Nile green tape. The petals go in pairs, i.e. the ones bending in are side by side and the ones bending out are also beside eachother. Keep the tips of the stamens about 4 -5 mm high in the centre of the flower.

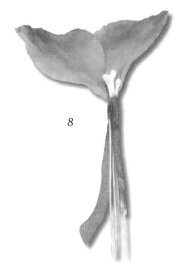

8

9

9. Roll a small slim cone of paste and attach to the stem at the base of the flower. Cut out a flat calyx and colour dark aubergine and burgundy. Attach to the stem of the flower pressing the petals up to cover over the slim cone. Leave to dry.

Leaves

Use the narrow metal leaf cutters and make a selection of leaves on 30/28g wire. Colour mid green and vein down the centre with a cel stick. Shape and leave to dry.

Assembly

Make a stem by taping a group of buds to a 20g wire.
Attach a few open flowers below the buds and around
the stem. Tuck a couple of small leaves under the
first group of flowers. Tape larger leaves at 1 - 1.5cm
intervals down the wire. Make a second small stem of ju
a group of buds in various stages of opening with leaves
Attach this group to the main stem.

CAMELIA (Japonica)
Silver Anniversary

I am constantly amazed by how many different variations of a single flower there can be. I have 2 species of Camelia and my neighbour Lesley, has 3. All are quite beautiful but vary considerably in their form. A substantial flower with delicate petals, this camelia holds it's own amongst the Helleborus and Spirea all jostling for attention along the right hand side of the garden path.

Equipment
Rose Petals KB 0519
Freesia cutter KB A006
Camelia petal veiner SKG

Materials
White & green porcelain paste
Medium stamens - Norma's noblies white
Nile green and white tape
28 & 26g white wires
Colours: yellow, cream and greens

Stamens

1. Twist a piece of ½ width Nile green tape between your finger and thumb into a tight length of about 4cm. Make 3 and tape them together onto a 28g wire. Give the tips a gentle curl.

2. Bunch together approx 40 medium stamens. Paint the tips of the stamens with yellow dust mixed with water. Feed the green stamens down through the centre of the bunch until they are just above the yellow ones. Over tape the stamens to the wire at the base to secure further.

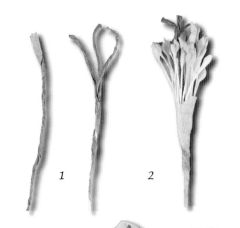

1   2

Petals

3. Roll out some fine white paste, Using the small cutter of the set, cut out a petal and insert a 28g white wire. Elongate it slightly and cut a small V in the top of the petal then soften around the edges and vein. Cup slightly and leave to dry. It takes approx 20 -23 petals to make a full flower. I use the same cutter for all the petals by stretching the paste with the ball tool before veining to make the outer petals a little larger.

4. Tape down the stems of each petal 1cm and attach tightly to the base of the stamens with ¼ width Nile green tape, interlinking the petals as you move around the flower.

3

4

Calyx

5. Roll out some green paste and cut 1 flat calyx using the freesia cutter. Make a Mexican hat and cut out another calyx. Soften the edges and slightly stretch the individual sepals to a point. Place the flat calyx onto the Mexican hat and secure. Make a hole in the centre and insert the main flower. Dust the calyx with green and a touch of light brown.

5

Buds

6. Roll a cone of white paste. Mark down the sides with a cell stick and twist the cone. Either cut out a small calyx or snip around the base with scissors to give the impression. Dust the calyx green.

6

Leaves

Use the Rose leaf or Hydrangea leaf cutter to make a selection of leaves in various sizes. I have veined these by hand using a leaf from the plant in the garden. However, A simple central vein from top to bottom with thin slightly wiggly veins going off to the side will do. Colour with dark green, mixing in some brown and yellow on the edges and finish with a gloss shine.

Assembly

Tape the flower to the top of a 22g wire adding in a bud just below. Tape the leaves close to the neck of the flower .

GOLDENROD

A flowering perennial which offers
a ray of sunshine on the darkest of
days. From late Spring to well into
Autumn the rich yellow flowers on
long swaying stems, travel through
a rainbow of golden shades - just
like the highlights in my niece
Emily's hair.

It has many different species but
all spread like wildfire and mine
fortunately covers up a multitude
of undesirables in the flowerbed -
phew!

Equipment
Ball tool, ceramic veining tool
Scissors
Calyx KB A002
Wallflower leaf cutter KB A014

Materials
Pale yellow and green porcelain
30, 28 and 20g green wire
Nile green tape
Tiny seed head stamens
Colours: strong yellows and a mix
of greens

Buds - for the top of the stem

1. Roll several small ovals of pale green porcelain varying in size from 3 - 5mm. Glue and insert a 30g wire. Snip the very tip of the larger buds with a pair of scissors. Dust the tip with yellow (to represent the petals inside) and dust the rest with light to medium green. Dust the smaller buds fully green.

Opening buds

2. Roll a small ball of pale yellow porcelain. Glue and insert a 30g wire. Cut out a petal with the midi calyx, soften the edges and roll over with a ridged cel stick.. Glue the ball and insert it down through the petal. Pinch the petals together around the ball with your fingers. Snip around the base of the bud with scissors to act as a calyx. Over dust the bud with deep yellow and the bottom snipped calyx with green.

Full flowers

3. Tape 4 tiny stamens to a 30g wire. Lightly glue the stamens and dip them into yellow pollen. Roll a small ball of pale green porcelain and insert the stamens down through the centre and secure.

4. Roll out some thin yellow porcelain, cut out a petal with the larger calyx KB A002. Soften and spread the edges with a ball tool and ridged cel stick. Cup in the palm of your hand. Dust with strong yellows.

5. From a Mexican hat of green porcelain and cut out a small calyx. With a little glue, place the yellow petal in the centre on top of the calyx and insert the stamens down through the centre and secure. Put a little glue around the base of the stamens if required. Tease the petals upwards. Dust the inside of the petals close to the stamen with a touch of light green and touch up the petals with more yellow if needed. Dust the calyx with greens.

Leaves

6. For the little leaves around the top of the flower, roll a thin cone of green paste, insert a glued 30g wire. Squash the paste flat between your fingers in the shape of a small leaf. Draw a line down the centre with a veining tool.

7. For larger leaves, use the wallflower leaf cutters, soften and spread the base of the leaf out a little, cup and then vein as above.

Assembly

Tape a group of mini buds together interspersed with a few very small leaves and attach onto the top of a 20g wire. Tape a few of the larger buds mixed in with a couple of open flowers into a group and onto the stem. Add 3 larger leaves at the base of the group of flowers. Continue down the stem at regular intervals to create a striking stem of your very own Goldenrod!

MAGNOLIA STELLATA

Twigs, flowers and furry buds, this Magnolia really stood out like a sore thumb with no foliage when I looked at it! The flowers are extremely delicate, very fine white petals with just a hint of pink in places. It almost looks a little naked beside the lush foliage of the camelia nearby. Needs protection from frost and also does not like the sun if it is too bright in the morning!

I had to include this as my Magnolia is still a small tree with not many flowers and I'm slightly worried it may not make it through the winter!

Equipment
Ball tool, scalpel, scissors
Magnolia Petal cutters – KB A010
Magnolia Petal veiner SKGI
8 petal daisy cutter KB A005

Materials
White and pale green paste
22 & 28g white wire
Nile green & twig florist tape
Colours: pinks, light & mid green, cream, yellow and a little peach and brown.

Buds

1. Roll a slim cone of white paste about 4-5cm long. Insert a glued 22g wire and secure.

2. Cut out 3 white petals, soften the edges and vein. Dust lightly with shades of pink at the tip and down the centre.

3. Glue around the central cone and place the base of the first petal at the bottom so it extends beyond the top. Wrap it around the cone leaving it slightly open at the top. Glue over the join of the first petal and place the second petal to the right of the join, wrapping around to the left, again leaving it slightly open.

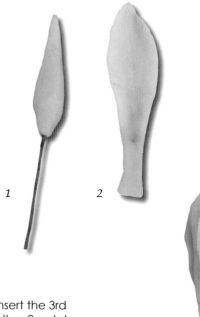

1   *2*

4. Place a little glue on the inside of the open 2nd petal and insert the 3rd petal as before wrapping it around to secure. Repeat for another 3 petals and attach with a little glue at the base of the bud, folding the petals inward but not too tightly, so they look as if they are opening up. Leave to dry

3 & 4

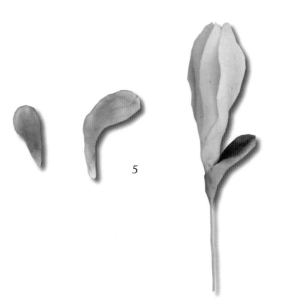

5

5. Roll a cone of green paste approx 2cm. Pinch the top into a plump seedpod shape. Place the rest of the cone against the side of the stem at the base of the bud and spread the paste around the stem securing with a little glue. Dust with light green and brown.

Flower stamens

6. Make a thin cone of white paste 1.5cm long. Glue and insert a 28g white wire, use scissors to snip around the outside and dust with light green and yellow.

7. Cut out 3 small white daisy shapes and divide each petal in half with a scalpel. Dust with pale peach and brown. Insert the cone down through the centre of the first daisy, glue and secure at the base of the cone. Repeat for the next two daisies. Leave to dry.

6　　　*7*

Petals

8. Cut out 6 small and 6 large magnolia petals from white paste. Glue and insert a 28g white wire to each petal. Soften the edges and vein. Dust with a mix of pale soft pinks and lilacs, making the smaller petals slightly darker in colour towards the top of each petal. Tape 2cm down each stem with ¼ width Nile green tape. Bend the wire at the base of the small petal into a slight curve inwards. Shape the outer petals backwards and leave to dry.

8

9. Place the 6 smaller petals around the base of the stamen and tape to the stem positioning the petals quite upright. Place the 6 larger petals in between the smaller petals and around the stem in a more open, falling back position. Secure with Nile green tape.

10. Add a seed pod as at step 4 and tape the rest of the stem with ½ width twig coloured tape. Make a number of flowers at different stage i.e. full petals and some as just a centre after the petals have fallen.

9　　　*10*

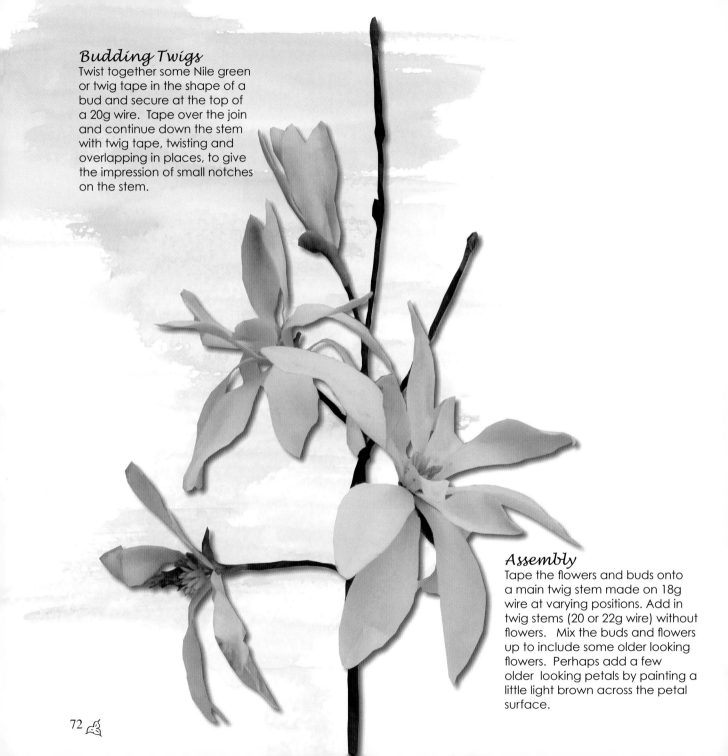

Budding Twigs

Twist together some Nile green or twig tape in the shape of a bud and secure at the top of a 20g wire. Tape over the join and continue down the stem with twig tape, twisting and overlapping in places, to give the impression of small notches on the stem.

Assembly

Tape the flowers and buds onto a main twig stem made on 18g wire at varying positions. Add in twig stems (20 or 22g wire) without flowers. Mix the buds and flowers up to include some older looking flowers. Perhaps add a few older looking petals by painting a little light brown across the petal surface.

HELLEBORUS 'ORIENTALIS'

This is a beautiful complex evergreen flowering shrub. At each stage of growth the flower is different, displaying an intricate formation of stamens and seed pods. In January at a time of only budding trees, it is glorious coming into bloom in the shade of the garden shed and seems happy to gently nod it's deep aubergine flowers in tune with the cool morning breeze.

Equipment
Ball tool, tweezers
Helleborus Set Cutters A001
Peony veiner SKGI
Tree Peony leaf veiner SKGI
Helleborus leaf cutters KB A017
Multi purpose leaf cutters KB A09

Materials
Dusky pink, white and green paste
30, 28 & 26g green wire
Hammerhead stamens (small and medium cream or pale yellow)
Longhead stamens (white)
Nile green florist tape
Colours: aubergine, yellow, light green, burgundy shimmer

73

Buds

1. Roll a cone of dusky pink paste 1.5cm in length. Hook, glue and insert a 28g green wire. Using a scalpel or frilling tool mark 3 or 4 lines from the top of the bud to the base. Dust with aubergine and burgundy colour dusts. Tape stem 3cm with Nile green tape.

1

Open full flower centre - stage 1

2. Paint the wire of 3 longhead stamens (representing carpels) with aubergine leaving the tip of the head white. Use full width white tape and secure around the centre a group of 30 small hammerhead stamens. Cut the group in half through the tape. Add 6 medium hammerhead stamens to the bunch keeping the small stamens at the bottom with the medium slightly raised above them and include the 3 longhead stamens rising out of the centre. Tape these onto a 26g wire with ½ width Nile green tape.

2

3

3. Using the KB A008 cutter, from green paste cut out 3 honey leaves. Use the ball tool to make one petal larger than the other two. Soften the edges and cup each sepal. Dust with mid green and edge with a little aubergine. Sit the petals inside each other - use a dab of glue between each - and thread the stamens down through top and secure. Curl the petals in towards the stamens.

4. Make a Mexican hat of green paste and cut out one more honey leaf. Soften the edges, cup, dust as the others. Make a hole with a cel stick and insert the stamens down through the centre. Secure with a little glue to the other petals and to the wire, pinching off any excess paste that is not needed on the stem. Leave to dry.

4

Developing seed pods (carpels) - stage 2

5. Make 3 small ovals of white paste 1cm in length. Pinch down the edge of one side and flatten slightly the opposite side. Insert a 30g green wire up through the pod close to the flattened side and out about 2cm from the top. Tease a little paste up the wire. Dust the pinched edge with light green. Dust the rest of the pod with aubergine. Make these of the same size, so they will fit neatly against each other. Tape the three together with ¼ width Nile green tape. Bend the extended wires out slightly from each other. Add a little green hip to the base. Leave to dry.

Make the honey leaf centres as at Steps 3 & 4 only - without stamens. Insert the pods down through the centre of the petals and secure with Nile green tape. (See flowers centre at the bottom of the page.)

For a variation on this you can make Full seed pods (carpels) - stage 3. Follow step 5 only making the pods slightly larger and fatter - no honey leaves. See photo on p76 for all examples.

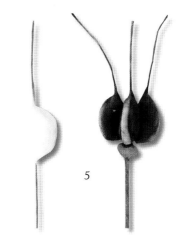

5

Flower petals (sepals)

6. From dusky pink paste cut out 5 petals. Insert a 28g wire soften the edges and vein. Tape all petals with ¼ width Nile green tape and dust the tape with a touch of aubergine to blend.

7. For fading flowers dust petals with a touch of light green at the top, sides and at the base by the stem. Dust the rest of the petal with a mix of grape violet, aubergine and burgundy shimmer. These petals are now opening up so shape bending the petals outwards slightly and leave to dry.

8. For new flowers dust the petals deeply with grape violet or aubergine mixed with a touch of black in the centre of the petal to add depth. Cup the petals inwards by placing it in the palm of your hand and leave to dry in shape.

9. Tape the petals tightly around the base of the centre or seed pods with ½ width tape. Dust the tape. Tape the flowers and buds onto an 18g wire using twig tape, dusting the green stems of the flowers with a little brown as it meets the stem.

6   7   8

9

Assembly

Tape the buds, leaves and flowers onto a 20g wire using Nile green tape dusted with aubergine to blend. Use twig tape as the stem gets thicker. Use the multi-leaf set to make a couple of small leaves to place behind the buds.

HELLEBORUS DOUBLE VISION

Another graceful example of Helleborus is this lovely double vision. It opens up into a large flower with multiple petals shimmering like silk and ranges in colour from white to cream to lime yellow.

The picked heads make an effective table decoration floating in a shallow bowl of water.

Equipment
Ball tool, tweezers
Helleborus Double Vision cutters KB A007
Helleborus leaf cutters KB A017
Helleborus leaf veiner SKGI
Peony veiner SKGI

Materials
Cream and pale green paste
30 & 28g white wire
Nile green florist tape
Colours: mixed greens, yellow cream
and brown, plus brown paint

Centre seed pods (carpels)

1. Make 3 small ovals of white paste max 1cm in length. Pinch down the edge of one side and flatten slightly the opposite side. Insert a 30g white wire up through the pod close to the flattened side and out about 1.5cm from the top. Tease a little paste up the wire. Dust the whole pod with light green carrying on up the wire. Dab a touch of brown paint on the tip of the wire. Make these the same size, so they will fit neatly against each other. Tape the 3 stems together with ¼ width Nile green tap. Bend the extended wires out slightly from each other. Leave to dry.

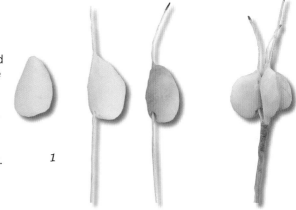

1

Petals

2. Cut out 8 of the smaller petals from cream paste. Glue and insert a 28g white wire. Soften the edges and vein. Dust with a mix of pale green and cream. Shape and leave to dry. Add a little brown to some of the edges of the older petals.

3. Cut out 12 larger petals and repeat step 2.

2

3

4. Tape the smaller petals tightly around the centre pods with ¼ width Nile green tape.

5. Add the larger petals around the outside of the smaller petals filling in any gaps. Continue until you have a full flower in an even shape.

4

5

Leaves

Make a selection of leaves as for the Argutifolius on p82. Vein and dust with light to medium shades of green to complement the paler colour in the flowers. Tape 2cm down the stem with ¼ width Nile green tape.

Assembly

Tape the flowers to a 20g wire with ½ width Nile green tape interspersing with leaves.

HELLEBORUS - ARGUTIFOLIUS

A cheerful addition to the garden
is this sweet Helleborus with
clusters of multiple cup shaped
flowers. Happily growing in the
shade or the sun, each year it
spreads itself a little further
across the flower bed! With
petals ranging from cream
to strong lime green it
stands out from the crowd
almost with a halo over
its head.

Equipment
Ball tool, tweezers, scalpel
Helleborus cutter KB 0185
Single Petal Blossom KB A001
Rose Petal veiner SKGI
Honyesuckle leaf veiner SKGI

Materials
Pale cream and goosberry green paste
30, 28 and 20g white wire
Colours: Greens, yellows and creams with a
touch of brown. Brown paint.

Buds

1. Make a small cone of cream paste max 1cm long. Glue and insert a 30g wire. Dust light green and leave to dry.

2. Cut out 7 small petals with the apple blossom cutter, soften with a ball too and vein on your hands. Cup slightly.

3. Glue over the green cone and lay 3 petals over it, inserting each one under the right hand open flap of the one before. Dab a little glue around the base of these petals and use the remaining 4 petals to surround the ball in the same way. Dust with pale green and cream and leave to dry. Tape stem 1cm with ¼ width Nile green tape.

4. Make some larger buds in the same way with a slightly bigger cone and using the small Helleborus cutter for the petals

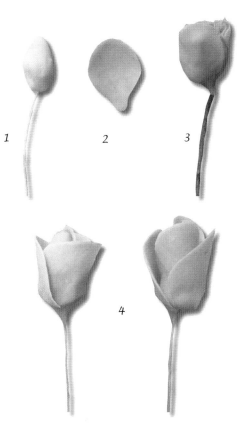

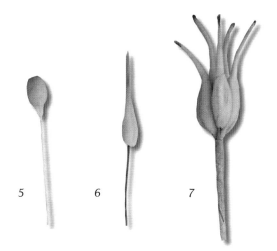

Flower Centres - seeds

5. With a small pea size piece of cream paste, make a cone and insert a 30g wire up through the middle and out of the top about 1.5cm.

6. Very finely roll the paste between your finger and thumb up the wire leaving the bulk of the paste at the bottom. Flatten one side of the base and pinch an edge on the other with tweezers. Bend the extending wire back slightly. Dust with light green and paint the tip of the wire with brown. Make 5 equal in size.

7. Glue the flat edge and put a little also on the side of each pod and join together in a group of 5. Tape with ¼ width Nile green tape.

Petals

8. Cut out a Helleborus petal, insert a glued 30g white wire, soften the edges, vein and cup with a ball tool. Dust with shades ranging from pale yellow mixed with light green to slightly darker greens. Leave to dry. Tape stems with ¼ width Nile green tape. Make 5 petals per flower.

9. Slightly bend the wire at the base of each petal and tuck under the group of seed pods securing with ¼ width Nile green tape.

8

9

Make some flowers with gooseberry green and some with cream porcelain as a base colour.

Leaves

10. From pale cream paste and using some small rose leaf cutters, cut out several leaves. Glue and insert a 30g white wire, soften the edges and vein with a honeysuckle veiner using very light pressure. Dust with pale green, cream and yellow to match the flowers and tape just below the head of the flower.

11. Use both sides of the second cutter to make a left and right angled leaf. Snip around the edges with a scalpel or scissors. I used a leaf from the garden for veining (see p7). Colour with mid to dark green cream and yellow highlighting the edges with a touch of brown.

10

11

Assembly

Tape all the flowers into groups of 2/3 flowers and buds. Tape these groups onto a 22g wire leaving approximately 2 -3 cm of stem between each. Add in smaller leaves throughout and place the larger leaves at the bottom of the whole stem.

ESCALLONIA

A hardy and pretty shrub which thrives on living by the sea. There are 2 well established plants at The Yews a red one and a pink one. From April to August they are full of buds developing into 5 petal blossoms, surrounding themselves in a blaze of colour before the petals fall leaving behind an interesting calyx and seed pod.

Equipment
Ball tool, scissors
Small single daisy petal cutter
Small calyx KB C005 or star cutter
Ball point pen

Materials
White and green porcelain
30g green wire
Small yellow seed head stamen
Small black Norma's Noblie stamen
Nile green tape
Colours: pinks, greens, yellow & brown dusts and red paint

Buds

1. Roll a small teardrop of white paste. Glue and insert a 30g wire in the narrow end. Gently snip around the neck of the bud to create a calyx. Dust the tip of the bud with pink and around the calyx with green. Lightly paint the tips of the calyx with red by mixing red colour dust and water.

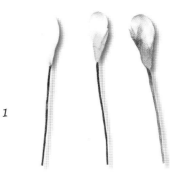

1

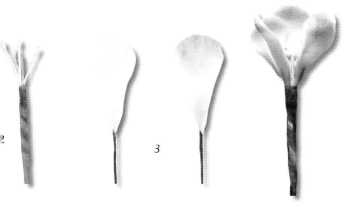

Flowers

2. Tape 4 yellow and one green stamen onto a 30g wire with ¼ width Nile green tape.

3. Cut out 5 petals from fine white paste. Insert a 30g white wire, soften the edges on your hand and cup slightly. Top and tail with a little pink. Tape together around the stamen with ¼ width tape.

3

4. Roll a Mexican hat and cut out small calyx or star. Dust with green and a hint of red. Insert the flower down through the calyx and secure.

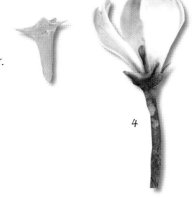

4

5. To make an old calyx after the petals have fallen, cut out a star from a Mexican hat, use an empty ball point pen casing and indent a circle into the top of the star. Insert a cut off black stamen and colour the calyx as before.

5

Leaves

Make small cones of green paste in various sizes. Insert a 30g wire and squash between your fingers. Draw a line down the centre of the leaf and colour dark green. Vary the shape of the leaf from a rounded top to a pointed one. My Escallonia in the garden seems to have both shapes of leaves.

Assembly

Tape some buds onto a 24g wire interspersing with leaves as shown, Add in flowers and an old calyx as you move down the stem. Make a few small branches and add them to the main stem.

PIERIS - Forest Flame

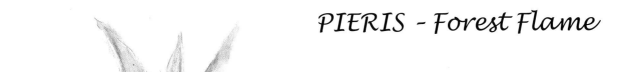

In a flower bed at the front of the house is this striking shrub. The young foliage is bright red, becoming pink and cream then finally green, with small cream bell-shaped flowers in large branched clusters in spring. I have recently discovered that 'Forest Flame' is a large evergreen shrub which can grow to 4m x 2m .... I may have put it in the wrong place!

Equipment
Ball tool
Metal leaf cutters KB A020
Black Bryony Veiner SKGI

Materials
Cream paste
30 & 26g white wire
Nile green florist tape
Colours: melon, red, cream, yellow and mixed greens
Gloss varnish

Leaves

1. From cream paste cut out several leaves of each size. Glue and insert a 30g white wire, soften the edges and vein. Colour as described, shape the leaves bending backwards and leave to dry.

Red foliage

Use yellow and cream up through the centre vein and melon mixed with a red around the outside. Shape and leave to dry.

Green foliage

Use shades of mid to darker green with a touch of yellow and cream.

Pale Green Foliage

Use pale yellow and cream at the top with darker greens towards the stem.

1

2. When dry, add a touch of brown paint along the edge and on the surface of some of the leaves or make a small tear in the leaf and paint brown around the edge.

3. Twist a little Nile green tape into a point and secure to a 26g wire.

2

3

4. Tape in the smallest leaves at the top of the wire with ¼ width Nile green tape. Add in larger leaves neatly below making a group of between 5 -9 on one stem. Make the stem 4 – 5 cms long in total. Make 3 stems.

4

Right - Cold porcelain Pieris tucked into the real shrub.

Assembly

5. Tape 3 of the red stems together. Twist Nile green tape into a point 1.5-2cm long and secure to the base of the joined stems. Paint the tips of tape with brown.

6. Tape on the green foliage around the stem. Add a 24g wire if you require more length. Varnish with ½ strength confectioners varnish or spray gloss.

Notes

Sometimes I go back to make a flower I have made in the past, and can't remember out of the numerous cutters that I have, which one on earth I used! The same goes for the colours and so here is a little space for you to jot down some notes which may be helpful to you.

Notes *cont ..*

Suppliers

KIT BOX
Metal stainless steel cutters
Unit 3 Neads Court
Knowles Road
Clevedon
Somerset BS21 7XS
www.kitbox.co.uk
support@kitbox.info
01275 879030 tel/fax

Tårtdecor Sweden AB
Everything you need
www.tartdecor.se
Utmarksvägen 18
442 39 KUNGÄLV
+46 0303 51470 tel
+46 0303 243099 fax

A Piece of Cake
Porcelain and all equipment
18 Upper High Street
Thame
Oxon O89 3EX
www.sugaricing.com
sales@sugaricing.com
01844 213428 tel/fax

Fine Cut
Metal Tin plate cutters
Workshop 4
Old Stable Block
Holme Pierrepont Hall
Nottingham NG12 2LD
www.finecutsugarcraft.com
info@finecutsugarcraft.com
0115 9334349 tel/fax

Squires Kitchen
Great Impressions veiners
The Grange
Hones Yard
Farnham
Surrey GU9 8BB
www.squires-shop.com
customer@squires-shop.com
0845 6171810 tel
0845 2255673 fax
+44(0)1252 260260 overseas

The Sugar Mill
Colour Dusts and Liquids
www.thesugar-mill.co.uk
01773 570737 tel

ARRANGEMENTS

I am certainly no florist and it is merely by trial and error that I have managed to arrange flowers into groups that I like! Sometimes less is more and therefore I find it better not to try to overfill a space just because I have flowers left over - let the flowers breathe.

I hope you are inspired by the following arrangements demonstrating the versatility of cold porcelain flowers

Left

A simple arrangement with stems of flowers just placed into an oasis.

Flowers included are:

Silver Birch Catkins
Pieris
Berberris
Double Red Poppies
Clematis
Sprigs of Wallflower
White and yellow
Poppy -variation on a
Himalayan Blue Poppy
Hydrangea Leaves

Right

A lovely dressing table arrangement in subtle colours of aubergine, cream, green and brown

Flowers included are:

Helleborus Orientalis
Helleborus Double
Vision
Grape Hyacinth leaves
The Bride buds and
seed pods

Left

In an attempt to make the spare bedroom pretty for my sister and her partner, I picked Hibiscus flowers from the garden and scattered them on the bed.

It took me 18 months to get the petal stains out of my best white linen!

Now I put porcelain flowers on the pillows instead. Here is a small spray of Hydrangea, Apple Blossom, Petiolaris and Escallonia - perfect for the occasion and a lovely gift for guests to take home.

Right

A Bridal Bouquet made using all the techniques included in this book

The large leaves have been taken from the Hydrangea in the garden, used as a template and a veiner.

On the actual wedding day, a Red Admiral butterfly paid the greatest compliment by resting on the central bloom.

Templates

Rose Petals / Apple
Blossom 0053 (3)

Berberris leaf A015 (3)

Lily of the Valley/
Berberris 0435 (2)

8 Petal Daisy
A005 (2)

Helleborus - Double Vision
A007 (2)

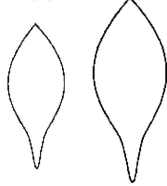

Apple Blossom A001 (2)
Hydrangea Petiolaris/The
Bride/Wild Marsh Flowers

Double Red Poppy / Himalayan
Blue Poppy A012 (3)

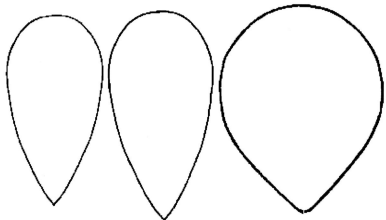

Christmas Rose/Helleborus
Argutifolius petal 0185

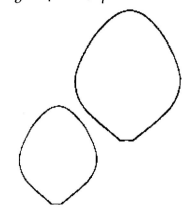

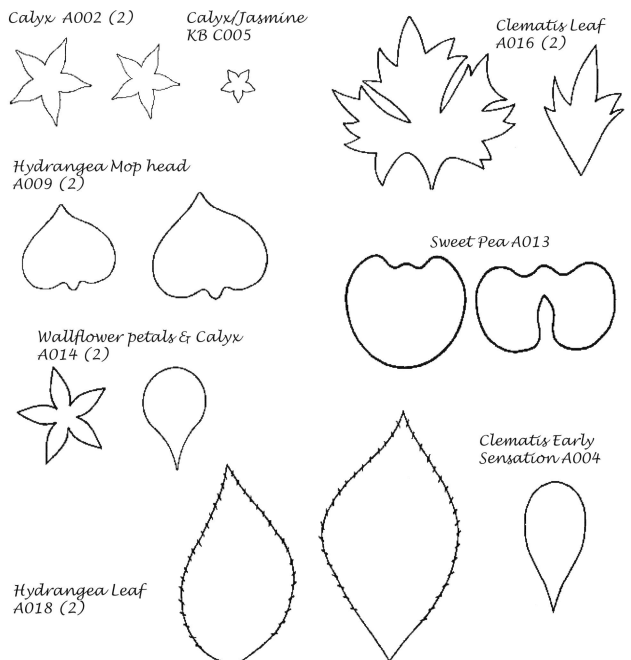

Calyx A002 (2)

Calyx/Jasmine
KB C005

Clematis Leaf
A016 (2)

Hydrangea Mop head
A009 (2)

Sweet Pea A013

Wallflower petals & Calyx
A014 (2)

Clematis Early
Sensation A004

Hydrangea Leaf
A018 (2)

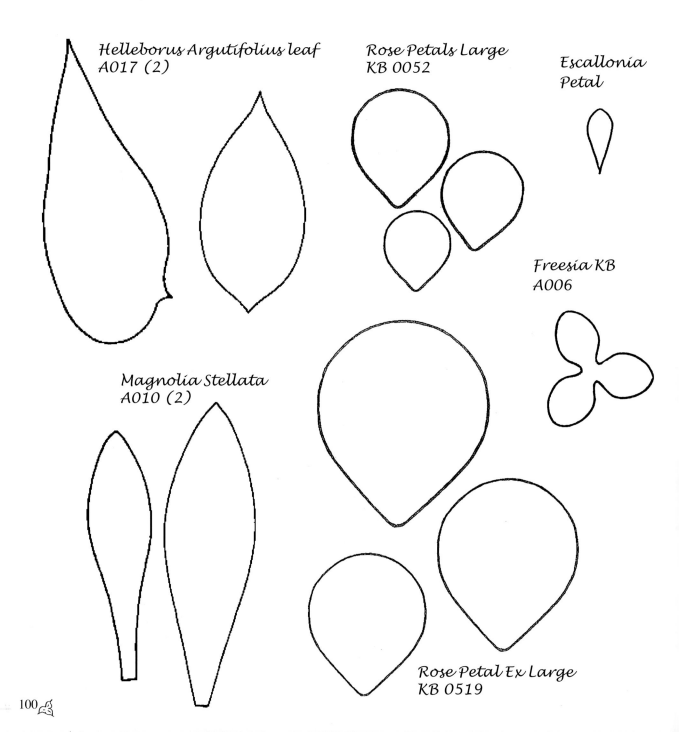

Helleborus Argutifolius leaf
A017 (2)

Rose Petals Large
KB 0052

Escallonia
Petal

Freesia KB
A006

Magnolia Stellata
A010 (2)

Rose Petal Ex Large
KB 0519

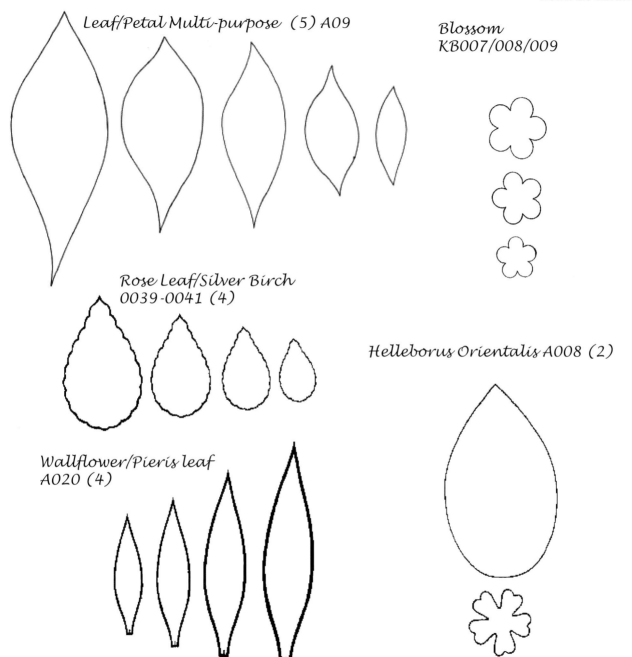

Leaf/Petal Multi-purpose (5) A09

Blossom
KB007/008/009

Rose Leaf/Silver Birch
0039-0041 (4)

Helleborus Orientalis A008 (2)

Wallflower/Pieris leaf
A020 (4)

Acknowledgements

Once again I would like to thank Dyck Willis of KIT BOX Cutters and his excellent team - especially Jackie - for all their help with the production and development of cutters to meet the requirement of this book.

To Beverly Dutton and the team at Squires Kitchen for their Great Impressions Veiners.

To my sons Peter and Felix who have done more than their fair share of cooking and ironing - although no harm done there!

To my dog Beth for keeping her legs crossed when I've said just another 5 minutes and we will go for a walk.

And finally, but most importantly my huge appreciation to Colin Brown and his team at MMS Almac Ltd, whose guidance, professionalism and attention to detail has encouraged and allowed me to produce this book from beginning to end in my own personal way.

Alyson R

If you would like to learn more about cold porcelain, arrange a demonstration or attend a workshop, please do not hesitate to contact me at alyson@alyson-reynolds.co.uk or visit the website on www.alyson-reynolds.co.uk

A Note from the Author ...

I hope that you have enjoyed the selection of flowers that I have chosen to include in this book. It has been my pleasure to share with you a little part of my garden and I look forward to meeting you again sometime in the future.

Best wishes